THE JAMESTOWN COLONY

BY CHARLES E. PEDERSON

Essential Events

THE JAMESTOWN COLONY

BY CHARLES E. PEDERSON

Content Consultant
David Givens
Senior Staff Archaeologist
Jamestown Rediscovery

ABDO
Publishing Company

CREDITS

Published by ABDO Publishing Company, 8000 West 78th Street, Edina, Minnesota 55439. Copyright © 2009 by Abdo Consulting Group, Inc. International copyrights reserved in all countries. No part of this book may be reproduced in any form without written permission from the publisher. The Essential Library™ is a trademark and logo of ABDO Publishing Company.
Printed in the United States.

Editor: Jill Sherman
Copy Editor: Paula Lewis
Interior Design and Production: Rebecca Daum
Cover Design: Rebecca Daum

Library of Congress Cataloging-in-Publication Data
Pederson, Charles E.
  The Jamestown Colony / by Charles E. Pederson.
     p. cm. — (Essential events)
  Includes bibliographical references and index.
  ISBN 978-1-60453-515-0
  1. Jamestown (Va.)—History—17th century—Juvenile literature.
2. Virginia—History—Colonial period, ca. 1600-1775—Juvenile literature. I. Title.

  F234.J3P43 2009
  973.2'1—dc22

                                          2008033108

TABLE OF CONTENTS

The Jamestown settlers arrived on ships such as these replicas.

A New Way of Life

In April 1607, the decks of several ships were crowded with men. They were studying the dark line of land far on the horizon. These men had traveled across the Atlantic Ocean from London, England, to reach Virginia.

When they glimpsed the unexplored shores of North America, they were undoubtedly excited to set foot on land again. These men were determined to make a new start in a new land. They had crossed the vast Atlantic Ocean on small ships. They had traveled thousands of miles, braving storms, sickness, and boredom. And they were among the first English people ever to see this stretch of coastline.

Forces in England

Over that past century, life had changed in England. This change had caused the travelers to make the decisions that brought them into this unfamiliar situation. Large landowners had begun to claim more land for themselves, and many people were forced from their farms. Harsh laws were created, aimed at keeping the poor under control of the rich. The poor were driven from the countryside and into large cities. The crowded city conditions bred

Mother of Presidents

Several U.S. presidents have come from Virginia. George Washington, Thomas Jefferson, James Madison, and James Monroe were Virginians. These men are sometimes called the Virginia Dynasty.

A total of eight Virginians have been president. In addition to the Virginia Dynasty, other Virginia-born presidents include William Henry Harrison, John Tyler, Zachary Taylor, and Woodrow Wilson. Virginia has earned the nickname, "Mother of Presidents."

disease and unemployment. As the cities grew, so did the problems. Some people began to look for opportunities in which they could start over and make a new life for themselves.

Spanish Armada

Although officially at peace in 1607, Spain and England shared a long history of unfriend-liness. In part, this was because England was a Protestant country and Spain was Roman Catholic. English ships that had raided Spanish ships and towns in the Americas heightened tensions. Spain's King Philip II intended to remove Elizabeth I from the English throne and take over England.

In 1586, King Philip began to gather an "Invincible Armada" of warships. It took two years to assemble and ready an armada of 130 ships that carried 27,000 men. Most of these were soldiers rather than sailors. England learned of Spain's plans and assembled its own fleet to meet the Spanish. They gathered approximately 200 ships with 16,000 men. Most of these men were experienced sailors.

Approximately two months of sailing brought the armada to the English Channel in 1588. Almost immediately, the English took the advantage by sending out fireships among the Spanish Armada. These gunpowder-filled ships were set on fire and sent to scatter the Spanish. After many losses in action, the armada was forced to return to Spain. On the way, a heavy storm destroyed approximately half of the armada.

In 1588, England experienced another change. The English had defeated an old foe, Spain. The Spanish had sent a huge fleet of ships to destroy the navy of Queen Elizabeth I. However, the English navy, aided by an unexpected storm at sea, almost completely destroyed the Spanish fleet.

This victory gave English sailors more confidence.

They were aware of the vast amounts of gold and land Spain had claimed in the New World of North America. The English wanted that wealth for themselves. Queen Elizabeth I gave some sailors permission to fight Spanish ships at sea and take their cargo. She gave others permission to establish colonies in North America. With her death in 1603, her successor, King James I, continued to challenge the Spanish for control of the wealth.

Shakespeare

Even playwright William Shakespeare felt the excitement of exploration. Though his play *The Tempest* takes place on an island, the land resembles Virginia as people pictured it in those days. "O brave new world / that has such people in't," wrote the playwright.[1] In the play, the characters' cultures clash. Shakespeare based his play on letters written by settlers at Jamestown.

Tales of a New World

This interest in exploration, along with the desire of the poor people of England to find new opportunities, set the stage for the establishment of an English settlement in North America. Excitement swept England as explorers began to tell tales of faraway, exotic locations and peoples. Many travelers exaggerated their stories, calling these places new paradises. Some explorers described Virginia as empty and ready. They said the land was ready to be farmed and that the native people could be converted to Christianity. The explorers often ignored the fact that most colonists died of disease, starvation, or conflict with native peoples.

THE VIRGINIA COMPANY

The Englishmen gazing at the Virginia shores were not concerned with events in England. Rather, they were preparing themselves to meet the challenges ahead.

These English voyagers arrived approximately 13 years earlier than the Pilgrims, who landed at Plymouth Rock. They also had a different reason to be there. The Pilgrims wanted religious freedom, but those who landed in Virginia in 1607 had their eyes on making a profit.

The Virginia Company of London had been important in getting the colonists to this point. People invested their money with the Virginia Company. In return, the company would send colonists to Virginia. These colonists were expected to find gold, silver, and other valuable resources and send their treasures back to London. These then would be sold at a profit for the Virginia Company investors. A group of wealthy men in London had created the Virginia Company, and they were eager to cash in on what they were hearing about the New World.

These travelers sent by the Virginia Company were about to found the first permanent English settlement in North America. They named it Jamestown, in honor of their king, James I. But the founding of the colony would be a difficult task and much more challenging than many of these men had imagined. They would face disease, starvation, hopelessness, and conflict. In her book, *1607*, author Karen Lange noted that Jamestown was a story of

> *suffering, of cruelty between English and Indians, and of thousands of unnecessary deaths. More than two-thirds of those who went to Jamestown between 1607 and 1625 . . . were dead by the end of the period.*[2]

Yet, Jamestown marked the birth of a new existence. It was the beginning of self-government.

British East India Company

The Virginia Company was not the only private British company to carry on foreign trade. In 1600, the British East India Company was formed to trade in the Far East. It gained trading rights in India from the ruling emperors. As the power of these rulers declined, local princes began to take company power away. The company tried to protect itself by getting involved in local politics.

The British East India Company grew in power until it ruled nearly all of India. In 1857, Indian troops rebelled against the company, and the British government took control.

It pioneered a mixture of cultures to form a unique, new way of life. "Most of all," says Lange, "Jamestown is a story about not giving up—about persevering."[3]

Pattern of Conflict

The Jamestown settlers would have frequent periods of conflict with Native Americans. According to Karen Lange in *1607*, the settlers' behavior set a pattern that lasted for many years to come. She writes, "Jamestown colonists fought the first of many wars that forced native peoples off their land. They started the first of many plantations that would eventually bring slavery to the South."[4]

An early map of the Jamestown settlement

Columbus sailed to the New World in 1492.

NEW LIFE IN A
NEW LAND

The English were not the first people to claim land in the New World. The Spanish and Portuguese had colonies in Central and South America. Some of these colonies dated back to 1492, the year Christopher Columbus made the first

Spanish claims in the Caribbean islands. In 1494, Spain and Portugal were Europe's two most powerful nations. They signed an agreement called the Treaty of Tordesillas. This agreement divided the known world into two parts at an imaginary boundary called the line of demarcation. Pope Alexander VI asked the nations to sign the agreement. He hoped it would keep the two empires from fighting over land.

Portugal claimed a huge area of what is now Brazil. Spain gradually gained control of nearly all of Central America. Its holdings included Mexico and most of the Caribbean, which was called the West Indies at that time. The Spanish also held power over southwestern North America. The western part of South America was similarly under Spanish control. Spain controlled vast natural resources, including gold and silver mines. These riches helped Spain become one of the world's superpowers. The access to these resources also attracted other countries, such as England and France, to the New World in search of wealth.

Saint Augustine

Saint Augustine, Florida, was founded in 1565 by Spanish explorer Pedro Menéndez de Avilés. It is the oldest permanent U.S. settlement established by Europeans. England gained control of Saint Augustine in 1763, but Spain reclaimed it 20 years later. In 1819, Florida became a U.S. territory, and Saint Augustine passed into U.S. hands.

In 1565, the Spanish established a settlement in Florida called Saint Augustine. The settlement served as Spain's navy headquarters for North America. The Spanish used it as a base for patrols that protected its ships from raiders. In 1570, Jesuit missionaries founded a settlement farther north along the coast by a large protected body of water on the Atlantic Coast. This area would become known as the Chesapeake Bay area. However, the Virginia Indians were not willing to aid or support the missionaries and killed them.

When the Virginia colonists arrived in 1607,

Privateers and Pirates

The Golden Age of Piracy lasted until the early 1700s. Queen Elizabeth I granted some of her subjects the right to steal Spanish treasure. These men were considered privateers, acting under the British government, and were protected by the might of English law. They included Sir Francis Drake and John Hawkins. A privateer is a private shipowner who has been commissioned by a government to work on its behalf.

Another group of sailors also attacked and stole Spanish treasure. These were pirates, or buccaneers. Although pirate activities sometimes appeared similar to the privateers', pirates did not act on behalf of a government. Their goal was personal wealth. They lived on Tortuga, Hispaniola, and other Caribbean islands.

Although the British government did not support piracy, if a pirate stole from the enemy, his actions were often overlooked. Some pirates returned to England and divided their goods with the government and were often pardoned. By the 1720s, the British navy put an end to most European pirate activity.

they were aware of Spain's claim on the area. Even though the Jesuit settlement had been abandoned, they were concerned that the Spanish might attack them and drive them away.

English Colonization

Spain had colonies in Central and South America since the early sixteenth century. Shortly after Spain's success in the New World, France began exploring the area and claimed much of North America along the northern Mississippi River and into present-day Canada. England attempted its first settlements in the New World in the 1580s. In 1584, Queen Elizabeth I gave Sir Walter Raleigh permission to establish a colony in the Chesapeake Bay area. Raleigh named the area Virginia in honor of Elizabeth, who, because she never married, was called the Virgin Queen. Raleigh sent

Walter Raleigh

Walter Raleigh began his career as an explorer under Queen Elizabeth's favor. She provided him with money, land, and permission to establish a colony in North America. He introduced the Indian potato plants and tobacco into England. During Raleigh's later life, he was in and out of Elizabeth's favor.

When James I became king, he believed Raleigh had opposed him. James imprisoned Raleigh in the Tower of London. He later was released to explore for gold in South America. Against orders, Raleigh attacked the Spanish. He was executed on October 29, 1618. Some historians, such as Stephen Greenblatt, have noted that Raleigh was not afraid to die. Greenblatt says Raleigh "joked with the executioner and even gave the signal for the ax to fall."[1]

several groups to start settlements. However, none of them succeeded due, in part, to lack of supplies.

One of Raleigh's colonies, known as the "Lost Colony," on Roanoke Island off the coast of modern North Carolina, remains a mystery. Raleigh sent a group to establish the "Cittie of Raleigh" on the Chesapeake Bay. The settlers landed on July 22, 1587. However, ships to provide additional supplies were unable to return to the island until August 17, 1590—three years later. Governor John White was a member of the supply group. He later wrote:

Spelling

Language changes over time. The way people spoke and wrote many English words in the 1600s would be almost unrecognizable to a modern English speaker. In addition, during the 1600s there was no standardized spelling of English words. Many people who wrote simply spelled words the way they pronounced them.

At our first [coming] to [anchor] on this shore we saw a great smoke rise in the [island of] Roanoak [near] the place where I left our Colony in the [year] 1587, which [smoke] put [us] in good hope that some of the Colony were there expecting my [return] out of England. [2]

The smoke may have been from Native American fires inland. It was not from the settlement, which had been abandoned. White reported that items had been "[thrown] here and there, [and were] almost [overgrown]

The Roanoke Colony was found abandoned in 1590.

with [grass] and [weeds]."[3] The only thing left behind were the letters CROATOAN carved into a tree.

White believed that Croatoan was a place with friendly Native Americans. He thought that the Roanoke settlers must have gone there. White tried to reach the area, but a storm forced his ship away from the coast.

Some researchers believe drought drove the colonists from their North Carolina homes. Others think Roanoke colonists left the island to live with nearby Native Americans. The settlers may have survived there for many years, but would have been killed in an attack by the Powhatan. This attack occurred shortly before Jamestown colonists arrived in 1607.

THE CHURCH OF ENGLAND

In the mid-1520s, the Roman Catholic Church denied England's King Henry VIII an annulment of his marriage to his Spanish wife, Catherine of Aragon. Henry VIII had asked the pope for the annulment in order to marry a younger woman, one who could bear him a male heir. Despite many pleas and arguments, the pope would not grant an annulment. King Henry split with Roman Catholicism and created the Protestant Church of England.

After the break from Rome, Henry VIII became the Supreme Head of the Church of England. He was then able to dissolve his own marriage to the queen and was free to remarry. Upon Henry VIII's death in 1547, the crown passed to his son Edward VI by his third wife. The Protestant Church of England continued as the official religion.

However, the next monarch was Henry VIII's daughter Mary. Her mother was his first wife, Catherine of Aragon, a Spanish Catholic. Under Mary, Catholicism once again became the official religion in England. In 1558, Henry's daughter Elizabeth by his second wife, Anne Boleyn, became the queen of England. The official religion of England became a blend of Protestantism and Catholicism. Queen Elizabeth I brought stability to England and reigned until 1603.

In the early 1600s, England experienced an increase in population and poverty. The peasants were losing their small plots of land. Lords began to charge rent for people to stay on their land. Many peasants could not afford to pay the rent and were forced off. Public grazing lands were fenced in for the wealthy landowner's use. The poor had nowhere to go. Some were put in prison as threats to society. Others were offered the chance to leave the country instead of staying in prison. Many became

Virginia Dare

On August 18, 1587, the first English child was born in America on Roanoke Island. She was named Virginia Dare. Because she was part of the "Lost Colony," nothing else is known about her.

indentured servants, working as unpaid help for a period of time, usually seven years. When Queen Elizabeth died in 1603, after ruling for more than 40 years, her cousin, King James VI of Scotland, became the new English king. He took the name James I of England and remained James VI of Scotland.

In 1607, 13 years before the Pilgrims left England to escape religious persecution, the men of the Virginia Company of London headed to the New World. They made the journey not for religious freedom but to search for riches and resources. ⌐

King James I was the leader of the Church of England.

Seal of the Virginia Company

REACHING VIRGINIA

In 1606, King James gave the Virginia Company of London a royal charter, or permission, to colonize the Chesapeake Bay area of North America. The Virginia Company intended to establish a settlement, search for gold, and start other moneymaking ventures. It claimed Virginia for the English crown.

The Virginia Company sent groups of men and workers to the New World. These men were chartered to look for gold and silver mines and claim land and raw materials. These resources would be sent to England, where the Virginia Company would sell them for a profit. In addition, the men were also asked to find a waterway to the Pacific Ocean, often called the Northwest Passage. The Virginia Company hoped that this route would replace the land passage to China, which was long and dangerous. China held desirable spices, silks, and other riches that the Company wished to trade for. Lastly, the colonists were to trade with the Native Americans, convert them to Christianity, and make them "civilized."

Many of these colonists were gentlemen. They belonged to wealthy families. The gentlemen at the Jamestown Colony were often the younger sons of these families. By English law, they could not inherit their father's property, which went to the oldest son at the time of the father's death. These gentlemen had few means of earning a living. Some became paid soldiers. Others became settlers, for example, in Jamestown. The men who went to Jamestown were called planters. Those who stayed in London and invested their money were called adventurers.

The Virginia Company outfitted three ships, the *Godspeed*, the *Discovery*, and the *Susan Constant*. The largest ship, the *Susan Constant*, was about 115 feet (35 m) long and 20 feet (6 m) wide. The smallest ship, the *Discovery*, was only 50 feet (15.2 m) long and 11 feet (3.4 m) wide. The ships carried 104 passengers and 39 sailors who were to set up the colony.

In 1606, the Virginia Company chose Christopher Newport as the convoy's commander. He had spent 20 years in Queen Elizabeth's navy and had battled the Spanish Armada. Newport would lead the expedition that founded the Jamestown Colony.

Company Charter

Over the years, King James authorized three charters for the Virginia Company. The first charter gave the Virginia Company all the land between the Atlantic and the Pacific oceans. The charter also stated that the Virginia Company should make Christians of the local people. But the major order to the Virginia Company was to "dig, mine, and search for all Manner of Mines of Gold, Silver, and Copper."[1]

SAILING TO VIRGINIA

The three ships of the Virginia Company left England on December 20, 1606. However, they did not sail directly from London to Virginia.

*The colonists were not able to sail directly from England
to the New World.*

They journeyed south past France, Spain, and
Portugal. At the Canary Islands in northern Africa,
they took on fresh supplies. The fleet then turned
west to catch favorable winds and tides that took them
across the South Atlantic to the Caribbean islands

and north past present-day Florida. After more than four months at sea, the ships entered the Chesapeake Bay on April 26, 1607. They sailed up and down the bay for several days, testing the water depth and seeking a favorable place to land.

The trip, like any ocean crossing of that time, was miserable. The ships were tiny, notes historian Michael Cooper, "with no more space than a typical classroom."[3] The food consisted of dried meat and hard biscuits. Their drinking water, fresh when they left port, quickly turned green from algae growing in it. Winter storms slashed at the tiny

A Storm at Sea

William Strachey, a Jamestown colonist, described a storm at sea in 1609:

For four-and-twenty hours . . . did we still find it not only more terrible, but more constant, fury added to fury, and one storm urging a second more outrageous than the former. . . . Sometimes shrieks in our ship amongst . . . passengers not used to such hurly and discomforts made us look one upon the other with troubled hearts and panting bosoms, our clamors drowned in the winds, and the winds in thunder. . . . It could not be said to rain: the waters like whole rivers did flood in the air. . . . I had been in some storms before. . . . Yet all that I had ever suffered gathered together might not hold comparison with this. There was not a moment in which the sudden splitting or instant oversetting of the ship was not expected. . . . In the beginning of the storm we had received likewise a mighty leak. And the ship . . . was grown five foot suddenly deep with water above her ballast, and we almost drowned within . . .[2]

ships alone on the vast waters. The ships leaked and water was constantly bailed from the bottom of the vessels.

Human relationships were also strained. Two of the expedition's leaders, John Smith and Edward Wingfield, had a serious argument. Wingfield accused Smith of trying to take over the mission. Because the Virginia Company had received permission directly from the king, such action would have been a serious crime. Smith protested the charges but was arrested and threatened with execution by hanging once they reached land. Smith was shackled for the rest of the trip.

THE GOVERNING COUNCIL

The Virginia Company had sent along a sealed box. It held the names of seven men who were to be the leaders, or governing council, of the settlement. Although many aboard the ship were aware of the

Newport's Later Life

Newport served for several years as a ship commander for the Virginia Company before joining the British East India Company. He died in late August 1617. *The Dictionary of American Biography* commented that most of Newport's fellow citizens appreciated him. Only John Smith had little good to say, including that he "speaks well of no one but himself."[4]

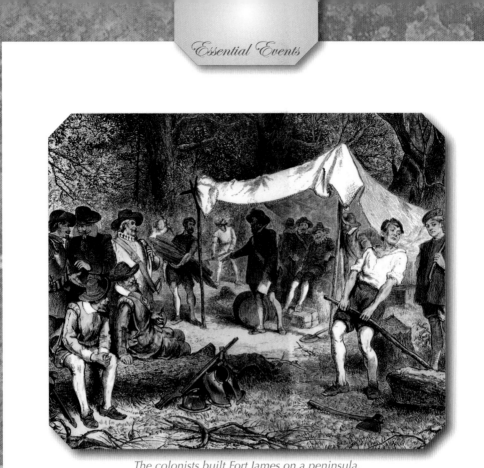

The colonists built Fort James on a peninsula.

box, it was not to be opened until the group reached North America. Once they arrived at Virginia, Newport opened the sealed box, and the names of the governing council were read aloud. These included Christopher Newport, Edward Wingfield, Bartholomew Gosnold, John Martin, George Kendall, John Ratcliffe, and John Smith. Even though Smith was a member of the leaders, Newport kept him prisoner a while longer.

On May 13, the three ships found a deepwater channel in a river approximately 60 miles (96.56 km) from the Chesapeake. They could anchor their ships close to shore for easy loading and unloading. On May 14, the group took up residence on what they thought was an empty island. They assumed that this area would be easier to defend than a spot on the mainland. They named a nearby river the James River. They called their encampment Fort James, and it would later become known as the Jamestown settlement. The names honored their ruler, King James I. Benjamin Woolley, a British historian, wrote, "In honour of their King, the council dutifully called the ramshackle collection of tents pitched on a sweaty island in the middle of a teeming forest 'Jamestown.'"[5]

What the men thought to be an island was actually a peninsula. The area had a higher section where they

John Smith

John Smith was born in 1580 in the village of Willoughby, England. When he was 16 years old, he left home. He became a soldier for the Dutch and fought for freedom from Spanish rule. He then worked on a trading ship, ending up in Austria in 1600. Later, he again became a soldier and fought the Ottoman Turks. In Hungary, the Turks captured him and sold him as a slave in Istanbul. Smith escaped from Turkey and returned to Eastern Europe. In 1604, he made his way back to England. He then became involved with the Virginia Company's plan to create an English colony in North America.

could watch for Spanish ships. The men continually feared attacks, so it was important to them to have a good defense.

However, despite the location's defensive advantages, it also had many negatives. The ground was low and swampy. The area was also prone to mosquitoes and other insects, which carried diseases. In addition, the area was already under the rule of another powerful nation—not Spain, but the Powhatan empire.

John Smith was one of the original colonists at Jamestown.

Colonists build the Jamestown settlement.

MISUNDERSTANDINGS

The English settlers had unknowingly chosen to settle in the middle of lands ruled by a powerful Indian leader called Powhatan. Powhatan ruled an empire of about 30 Native American groups. The English called these Native Americans

Powhatans after their paramount, or supreme, chief. His empire was based at Werowocomoco, about 15 miles (24 km) north of Jamestown. The Powhatan empire covered a vast area, approximately 10,000 square miles (25,900 sq km).

Although the English called the land "Virginia," it had a much older Indian name, *Tsenacomoco*. The Powhatan ancestors had arrived in the Tidewater area around the year 200. By 1600, an estimated 15,000 to 25,000 Native Americans occupied the Tidewater. Chief Powhatan ruled as many as 12,000 to 13,000 of these Native Americans. The Powhatan were farmers and grew crops of corn, beans, and squash all in a single field. They also were hunters and fishers.

The land must have seemed empty to the newcomers, but that was an illusion. All the land in the Virginia Tidewater area was used by the local Native Americans. In addition, the enemies of the Powhatan were pressuring them into the area where the English were trying to settle. The Monacans and Mannahoacs to the

Seemingly Empty Land

The English believed the land they settled on was empty. One reason, according to historian Karen Lange, may have been because "during the spring and summer and fall, many [Native Americans] would leave their villages in search of food. The small number of people in [Native American] villages during the warm months made Powhatan lands look uncrowded to the newly arrived English. But in reality the Indians were using every bit of space."[1]

west and the Iroquois-related nations to the north raided the Powhatan.

Powhatan History

The reservation of the Powhatan Renape Nation is based in Westampton Township, New Jersey. Chief Roy Crazy Horse has tried to educate people about the Powhatan Renape Nation and Indian culture. Crazy Horse explains:

We are the native natural people of this land, descendants of an ancient confederation that at one time included over thirty nations. Our people were placed here by the Creator, and have maintained an unbroken history of thousands of years of settlement along the coastal areas of the mid-Atlantic. Although most of our lands are now occupied by others, many of the nations of the original Powhatan Confederacy still survive. The oldest treaty written in this land is between the Powhatan Nations in the year 1646.

Since the time we met the Europeans in the 1500's, our history has been characterized as a struggle to survive war, disease, prejudice, and cultural disintegration. Foreign disease alone probably accounted for halving the Powhatan population by the end of the [1600s]. Many of the survivors of those early epidemics were largely decimated by war and starvation. Yet, against all odds, we the Renape (human beings) have survived.[2]

Prior to the English landing at Jamestown, the Powhatan had predicted a nation from the east would destroy the Powhatan empire. Chief Powhatan did not think the prophecy referred to the English. He connected the prediction to an Indian nation on the Chesapeake Bay. Powhatan ordered his warriors to kill this neighboring tribe so the prophecy would be unfulfilled.

COLONISTS AND POWHATAN

The Jamestown settlers were to explore the seemingly uninhabited area for the Virginia Company. They hoped to find valuable resources and other moneymaking opportunities for the investors in England.

Newport's orders were to sail up the James River as far as the first waterfalls, near present-day Richmond, Virginia. Newport and his crew left on May 21, 1607, for the heart of Powhatan territory. They encountered Native Americans along the river. The settlers and Native Americans traded goods and conversation. Some of the Native Americans hinted that more wealth was to be found in the higher land inland to the west. They also spoke of a "great salt water" far to the north and west. It may have sounded like it could be the waterway of the Northwest Passage. In reality, the description was probably of the Great Lakes. However, even these large waters would not provide passage to the Pacific Ocean.

At the falls, Newport's men put up a small cross with the Latin words *Jacobus Rex. 1607* (King James. 1607). The cross showed that the English claimed the land for their king. The cross angered Powhatan and other leaders. According to Christopher Woolley,

Newport tried to calm Powhatan by telling him that "the two arms of the cross signified King Powhatan and himself, the fastening of it in the [middle] was their united league."[3] Powhatan's son Parahunt was sympathetic to the English explorers. He told his people:

> *Why should you be offended with them as long as they hurt you not, nor take anything away by force? They take but little waste ground which doth you nor any of us any good.*[4]

This event marked the beginning of a strained relationship between the colonists and the Powhatan that alternated between peace and fighting for years to come. The Powhatan wanted the iron tools and the weapons of the English. The English needed food to survive. When the Powhatan thought the English were taking too much land, they sometimes attacked. If the English could not trade for food, they occasionally stole it.

On May 26, just weeks after the first English arrived on the Virginia coast, a group of 200 Native Americans attacked the settlers. The reason for the attack was unclear. They may not have liked strangers taking over their land. The English had not yet had a chance to build defenses or plant crops. At least

Colonists often fought with local Native American tribes.

one Englishman was killed and several more were wounded in the attack. But sailors met the attack with cannons. John Smith said that if it were not for cannon fire, "our men [would have] all been slain."[5]

The attack startled the settlers into action. They began to build a triangular fort by using upright logs called palisades planted into the earth. They placed several cannons on platforms at each corner. After some Powhatan were seen creeping close to their new fort through the long grass, the settlers cut the grass short. That way, they could see if the Powhatan were getting close. Several weeks later, Chief Powhatan stopped all attacks against the English. He also sent them meat. With things calmer, settler William Brewster called Virginia "the most stately, rich kingdom in the world."[6]

Newport would soon be leaving for the return sail to England. Some of the settlers had looked for gold. They brought back rocks for Newport to take to London, where they would be examined for gold. His ship was loaded with timber to sell as well. On June 22, Newport set sail for England. He had left enough supplies to last until October, but he warned the colonists that mid-November was the earliest he could return.

Despite the end of Powhatan attacks, the settlers continued putting up palisades in their fort. Then conditions quickly worsened. Colonists began to become ill with malaria, typhoid, and other diseases. The few crops that had been planted would not become ripe for many weeks, and Newport was not expected for months.

That summer, the settlers experienced a severe drought. The drought had begun around 1606, before the colonists had arrived. Many of the hardships the colonists endured during their first years at Jamestown were due to the lack of rain. Unable to raise adequate crops and without a supply of fresh water, hunger, sickness, death, and conflict plagued the settlers. According to archaeologist Dennis B. Blanton, the drought

> *also help[s] explain tensions between the English and Indians over corn supplies. It may not be a coincidence that the [two cultures got along better] in 1612 after the drought when corn supplies were more abundant. The tragic mortality rate in the colony is also better understood under drought conditions, a time when malnourished and thirsty colonists would be most vulnerable to sickness.*[7]

On September 10, Edward Wingfield was removed as the president of the council. Wingfield was one of the original investors in the Virginia Company. John Ratcliffe was elected president and served for the next year.

Wingfield Deposed as President

Edward Wingfield described how he was removed as president of the governing council: "The 10 of September, Mr Ratcliff, Mr Smyth, and Mr Martynn, came to the President's tent with a warrant, subscribed under their hands, to depose the President; saying they thought him very unworthy to be either President or of the Council, and therefore discharged him of both. He answered them, that . . . the President ought to be removed . . . by the greater number of 13 voices . . . [and] that they were but three, and therefore wished them to proceed advisedly. But they told him, if they did him wrong, they must answer it. Then said the deposed President, 'I am at your pleasure: dispose of me as you will, without further tumult.'"[8]

Copper Trade

Archaeologists who excavated the Jamestown site discovered that much trade in copper occurred between 1607 and 1609. After 1610, the trade dropped off. With so much copper being traded, it may have lost its value.

Smith became the principal trader with the Native Americans. The Powhatan wanted copper from the English. Copper was a very valuable metal to the Powhatan, because they used it for jewelry and trade.

But more than copper, the Powhatan wanted to obtain powerful English weapons. They were impressed by the power of the English cannons and rifles. The Powhatan could use these weapons to better resist their enemies. The English did not seem like much of a threat, so the Powhatan were willing to trade food to keep the English alive. They hoped that later they could obtain the English weapons.

John Smith was the principal trader with the Powhatan Indians.

John Smith's map of Virginia

The John Smith Era

The Jamestown colonists had been charged with the order to find the Northwest Passage to China. In December 1607, Smith and several companions left Jamestown to explore upriver. George Casson guarded their boat while the others explored on foot. Opechancanough, Powhatan's brother, and a group of his warriors captured Casson. Opechancanough was a powerful leader called a werowance (good person). He controlled the land between the Pamunkey and Mattaponi rivers.

Opechancanough brought Casson to his village, where he was interrogated and tortured. Even after Casson told them he was with Smith, the abuse continued. British historian Benjamin Woolley described the horrific scene. Using sharp shells and reeds, a Powhatan priest

> set about cutting through the flesh and sinews of Casson's joints. . . . As each of his limbs was removed, it was cast upon the fire, until only his head and trunk were left.[1]

The Native Americans also killed two other members of the party. The rest of the explorers returned safely to Jamestown.

The Northwest Passage

One of the goals of the settlers at Jamestown was to find the Northwest Passage, a shortcut to China. Europeans were eager to find a shortcut to China to avoid the long and dangerous crossing by land or around the southern tip of Africa. The settlers never found the route, nor did other explorers for many centuries.

There is a Northwest Passage, but until recently it has been covered by ice. Global climate change has melted the ice cap in Canada, and it is now possible to sail from the Atlantic to the Pacific Ocean.

JOHN SMITH AND POCAHONTAS

Opechancanough, however, captured John Smith. When Smith wrote of his capture later, he explained how he tried to defend himself:

> *The air was thick with arrows, some passing through [my] clothes but, miraculously, not [my] body. Using [my] guide as a shield, [I] fired [my] gun three or four more times, while attempting to make [my] way back to the river. Then [I] found [myself] surrounded by two hundred warriors—no, three hundred—[Indians] with bows drawn and arrows aimed.* [2]

Opechancanough took Smith to meet paramount Chief Powhatan, who gave Smith a big feast. Afterward, several fierce warriors dragged Smith over to two great stones. Smith believed the chief had ordered these warriors to kill him. According to Smith, just as the warriors were about to club his head against the stones, an

A Priest of the Powhatan

John White, a member of the supply group, described several of the original Virginia inhabitants. He described their priests, or werowances, as older and more experienced "then the [common sort]. They [wear] their [hair] cut like a [crest], on the [tops] of their [heads] as others [do], but the rest are [cut short, saving] those which [grow] above their foreheads. . . . They also have [somewhat hanging] in their ears. They [wear a short cloak] made of fine [hare skins] quilted with the [hair outward]. The rest of their [body] is naked."[3]

Pocahontas is shown saving John Smith from execution.

11-year-old girl named Pocahontas saved him from execution. Smith claimed that Pocahontas threw herself on him to stop the warriors from crushing his head. Afterward, Chief Powhatan told Smith that they were friends, and he adopted Smith as a subchief, or son. Smith was released after a month, and he returned to the Jamestown settlement.

Although this story of John Smith and Pocahontas has become famous, many scholars doubt the incident ever happened. These scholars cite an account that Smith wrote shortly after the event was said to have occurred. The account does not mention Smith's near execution. Smith did not write about it until many years later. Scholars suspect that this story was simply a way for Smith to make himself look good. Others say that if the incident did occur, it is likely that Smith misunderstood the rescue and that it was more likely part of a ritual.

Pocahontas, the young girl in the story, was a favorite daughter of Chief Powhatan. Her real name was Matoaka. Her nickname, Pocahontas, means "mischievous one." Pocahontas seems to have admired John Smith. She came to Jamestown often with messages or food to trade. She enjoyed turning cartwheels in the open square of the fort. Smith admired her and later wrote that she was the best-looking and most intelligent of all the Native Americans. The legend of Pocahontas says she and Smith fell in love, but this almost certainly was not the case.

Hunger and Illness

When Smith returned to Jamestown from captivity with Powhatan, he immediately ordered several wells to be dug inside the fort. He wanted a safe source of fresh water. Many of the colonists had died after drinking the river water, which was "at a flood very salt, at a low tide full of slime and filth," according to George Percy.[4] Typhoid and other bacteria in the water killed many settlers. Smith hoped that the new wells would help improve the health of the colonists. However, even with the new wells, people continued to become sick.

According to Percy, "Our men were destroyed with cruel diseases—as swellings, burning fevers—and by war."[6] Before these causes of death, however, the major cause was simply starvation.

THE FIRST SUPPLY

After ten months at the

Pocahontas from Modern Powhatan

Chief Roy Crazy Horse, of the Powhatan Renape nation, does not agree with the popular image of Pocahontas and John Smith's relationship. Like many historians, he believes that the story was either false or exaggerated. He writes:

. . . the first time John Smith told the story about this rescue was 17 years after it happened, and it was but one of three reported by the pretentious Smith that he was saved from death by a prominent woman.

Yet in an account Smith wrote after his winter stay with Powhatan's people, he never mentioned such an incident. In fact, the starving adventurer reported he had been kept comfortable and treated in a friendly fashion as an honored guest of Powhatan and Powhatan's brothers. Most scholars think the "Pocahontas incident" would have been highly unlikely . . .[5]

Typhoid

Typhoid is a disease that is transmitted when the bacteria in contaminated food or water is consumed. If left untreated, typhoid causes fevers, headaches, and stomach aches. Typhoid may cause open sores in the intestines called ulcers. If the ulcers result in holes in the intestines, the infection may become deadly. Ulcers can also cause a person to bleed to death. Throughout history, typhoid has killed thousands of people.

Jamestown settlement, the colonists were running low on supplies. Their attempts at farming had been unsuccessful, and they were forced to rely on trade with local Native American tribes to help them through the hard times. However, the settlers only had so much that they could trade. The desperate settlers did not know how long they could last or when Newport would arrive with supplies.

At last, Newport arrived at Jamestown on January 2, 1608, to deliver what is known today as the "First Supply." He commanded two ships with about 100 passengers.

Newport found only 38 of the original 104 settlers whom he had left behind six months earlier. The settlers were besieged by problems with their leaders. The former council president, Edward Wingfield, was in prison on suspicion of not following the Church of England. John Smith was set to be hanged for letting two of his exploration party be killed. Newport freed Wingfield and Smith and helped the colony get back on its feet.

On January 7, 1608, a fire raced through Jamestown and destroyed shelters and stores of food. The Powhatan came to the settlers' aid and brought them food supplies. Again, the settlers would have to rely on trade with the Powhatan to make it through the harsh winter. Newport visited paramount Chief Powhatan at his capital of Werowocomoco. After the winter, Newport left again for London on April 9.

From June through September, Smith explored Chesapeake Bay. He sailed the rivers that emptied into it. Smith was looking to trade with the local Native American tribes, but he was also looking for the Northwest Passage.

In September 1608, Smith was elected president of the Jamestown governing council. The settlers repaired the church and put up buildings to store supplies they expected on the next supply ship. Smith had the men train together with weapons as a militia. Learning

Ratcliffe's Palace

Ratcliffe had been building a "palace" in the woods, perhaps to impress the Native Americans. Smith stopped the work on Ratcliffe's project, calling it a "thing needlesse."[7] It had consumed too much time and labor.

from his past experiences, he informed the settlers, "He who does not work will not eat."[8] His strong leadership helped the colony survive and grow. ⌐

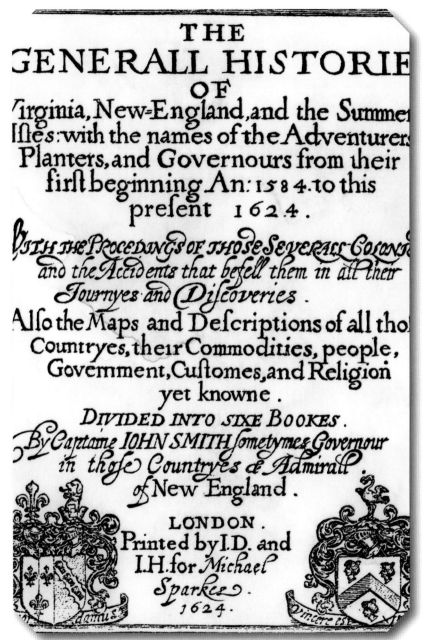

THE GENERALL HISTORIE

OF

Virginia, New-England, and the Summer
Isles: with the names of the Adventurers,
Planters, and Governours from their
first beginning An: 1584. to this
present 1624.

WITH THE PROCEDINGS OF THOSE SEVERALL COLONIES
and the Accidents that befell them in all their
Journyes and Discoveries.

Also the Maps and Descriptions of all those
Countryes, their Commodities, people,
Government, Customes, and Religion
yet knowne.

DIVIDED INTO SIXE BOOKES.

By Captaine IOHN SMITH sometymes Governour
in those Countryes & Admirall
of New England.

LONDON.
Printed by I.D. and
I.H. for Michael
Sparkes.
1624.

John Smith detailed the history of the Jamestown colony in his book,
General History of Virginia, New England.

The first women arrived in Jamestown in 1608.

THE STARVING TIME

In September 1608, Newport returned from England with the Second Supply and more settlers. He also brought with him the colony's first two women. There were also eight "glass men." They and other artisans would manufacture products that the Virginia Company could sell in England. Smith approved of the newcomers. During the summer, he had come to the conclusion that there was little gold, silver, or other precious metals to be found. He felt that their time would be better spent producing goods to sell in England.

The colony grew again when seven more supply ships arrived at Jamestown on August 11, 1609. This was the Third Supply. These ships carried as many as 300 men, women, and children. Men had brought their wives and children to the Jamestown colony. The Virginia Company investors hoped that the presence of women and children in the settlement would help make it a permanent colony. Previously, several of the Jamestown settlers had married Powhatan women. These unions had helped establish peace and understanding between the two groups. However, as more women arrived from England, the frequency of cross-cultural marriages decreased.

The Third Supply had an eighth ship, the *Sea Venture*. The vessel had been shipwrecked on its way from the

Smith's Later Life

Smith left Virginia for England in 1609. In April 1614, he returned to North America. He explored the coast of Massachusetts and Maine, naming the area New England. After this trip, he returned to England. He spent the rest of his life writing books. In 1631, he died at age 51.

Caribbean to Jamestown. The passengers and crew were forced to spend the winter in Bermuda and could not join the other supply ships.

In Jamestown, Smith was badly injured on a trading journey. Gunpowder that he carried in a pouch had exploded. It set his clothes on fire and burned his skin along one side. Describing the scene, Smith said that, to put out the blaze, "[I] threw [myself] overboard into the river, nearly drowning as [my] men struggled to pull [me] back into the boat."[1] Smith had expected to die but he survived.

Smith's injuries were still painful

George Percy

George Percy was born on September 4, 1580. Like several of the other Jamestown settlers, he had been in the military. Percy gained practical military experience in Europe while fighting for the Dutch.

In September 1609, Percy had been intending to leave Virginia when Newport made his return trip to England. Percy was ill and thought that he would regain his health more easily in England. However, when it became clear that Smith would be leaving, some of the other council members convinced Percy to stay. They wanted him to become the new president when Smith left.

Percy stayed in Jamestown, but he was the unfortunate president during the Starving Time. Some of the settlers blamed him for the colony's problems. However, there was little that Percy could do to help the settlement. The lack of food and the cold winter took its toll on his health; Percy was so ill that he could hardly stand.

Percy left Virginia in 1612. By 1625, he was again fighting for the Dutch. He died in 1632 at age 51.

in the fall of 1609, when Newport was preparing to return to England with settler-made tar pitch, glass, soap ashes, and other products. Smith decided to return to England with him. Newport and Smith left Jamestown in October. Smith would not return to the settlement.

With Smith's departure, George Percy took control as the president of the governing council.

Winter

The winter of 1609 to 1610 brought harsh weather and the Starving Time. The settlers had landed at Jamestown during a period of history with cooler than usual weather. Geologists have determined that during this period there was a global cooling, which they call the Little Ice Age.

Aside from freezing, the settlers had little food. They had not been able to grow and harvest many crops. They had not been able to tend the crops they had planted because of Native American attacks.

The settlers ate whatever they could find. Before the Starving Time, there had been a number of pigs in the settlement. The settlers ate every one of them. When the pigs were gone, they ate horses, dogs, cats, rats, and snakes. They ate local mushrooms that made them sick. One man was accused of eating his dead wife. (The man was later executed for the crime.) Many of the settlers died of starvation. Of the 500 settlers who started the winter, about 60 were left by spring 1610.

Cause of Death

Many settlers died from starvation and disease. Others seemed to die from lack of hope. George Percy wrote: "Others going to bed, as we imagined, in health, were found dead the next morning."[3]

New Beginnings

In the spring of 1610, the passengers of the missing supply ship *Sea Venture* arrived at Jamestown. William Strachey, one of the survivors who made it to Virginia, wrote:

> *We made up our longboat . . . in fashion of a pinnace [small boat], fitting her with a little deck made of the hatches of our ruined ship, so close that no water could go in her, gave her sails and oars.*[2]

A new leader, Thomas Gates, also arrived. The Virginia Company had been reorganized in London. They chose Thomas West, Lord De La Warr as Jamestown's new governor and Thomas Gates as deputy governor. De La Warr was unable to leave London right away, and Gates was sent to serve as acting governor until De La Warr's arrival.

Gates found the settlement in a desperate condition. He found the 60 colonists who had survived the difficult winter. These colonists were all in poor health. When Gates arrived, William Strachey wrote:

> *Viewing the fort, we found the palisades torn down, the ports open, the gates from off the hinges, and empty houses (which owners' death had taken from them) rent up and burned, [for firewood].* [4]

Gates did his best to restore the declining settlement, but it was no help. On June 7, 1610, he gave the order for the remaining settlers to board ship and leave Jamestown. On June 8, the departing settlers were surprised to meet a ship approaching Jamestown. Lord De La Warr, the new governor of Jamestown, had arrived with 300 men and more supplies. Gates ordered the ships to return immediately to Jamestown to try again.

Lord De La Warr

Thomas West, Lord De La Warr, served in the Dutch military. The Virginia Company chose him to be the first governor of Virginia. His expedition arrived just in time to stop the colonists from leaving Jamestown. He was in Virginia for nine months before he became ill. De La Warr left the colony to recuperate in the Caribbean. After he recovered, he returned to England.

In early 1618, he led another expedition for Virginia. Stopping at the Azores Islands off Africa, he and his entire crew became sick after a feast. Some historians believed they were poisoned. De La Warr died on June 7, 1618.

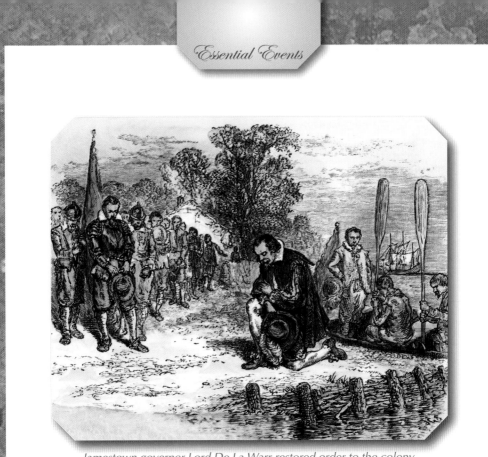

Jamestown governor Lord De La Warr restored order to the colony.

De La Warr made a grand entrance, as Strachey noted:

> Upon his lordship's landing at the south gate of the palisade . . . [De La Warr] marched up into the town, where at the gate I bowed with the colors and let them fall at His Lordship's feet, who passed into the chapel.[5]

The Jamestown settlers felt a renewed optimism as they began to repair Jamestown. The fort remained triangular. Two of its sides measured 140 yards (128 m) and 100 yards (91 m). At the corners they placed cannons. Each wall had a street of houses alongside it. At the center of the fort was a marketplace. A church stood there too.

CHANGING LEADERSHIP

Newport left Jamestown once again in July 1610, taking Gates with him. Less than a year later, De La Warr left Jamestown on March 28, 1611, because of poor health. With both Gates and De La Warr in England, former president George Percy assumed leadership as deputy governor until a new governor arrived.

On May 12, Newport arrived with a new supply and the new deputy governor, Sir Thomas Dale. To bring the settlement under control, Dale used harsh discipline. He controlled Jamestown until August, when Thomas Gates returned as the lieutenant governor. Gates brought with him 280 new settlers, six ships, food, and cattle.

Together, Dale and Gates ruled the colony with stern discipline. Settlers could be put to death for crimes such as theft or the slaughtering of animals for food without permission. When Gates eventually

Leadership of Jamestown changed hands many times. Originally, the colonists elected a president to serve as their leader. In 1609 the Virginia Company appointed a governor of the colony. However, because of frequent trips to London the leadership of the colony often fell to others:

• Edward Maria Wingfield (President, 1607)
• John Ratcliffe (President, 1607–1608)
• John Smith (President, 1608–1609)
• George Percy (President, 1609–1610)
• Thomas Gates (Lieutenant Governor, 1610)
• De La Warr (Governor, 1610–1611)
• George Percy (Deputy Governor, 1611)
• Thomas Dale (Deputy Governor, 1611)
• Thomas Gates (Lieutenant Governor, 1611–1614)
• Thomas Dale (Deputy Governor, 1614–1616)

left Jamestown again, Dale took control. He moved most of the settlement from Jamestown farther up the James River to Henricus. Native Americans already occupied the area, but the settlers fought them and forced them out.

Dale continued to enforce severe laws to bring harsh discipline to the settlers. If the settlers did not work, they would not receive food. Hangings, tortures, and other actions were common. George Percy wrote:

. . . one [person] for [stealing] of 2 or 3 pints of [oatmeal] had [a hair pin] thrust through his [tongue] and was [tied with] a [chain] to a tree [until] he starved. . . . Many through these extremities, being [weary] of life, [dug] holes in the earth and there [hid] themselves till they famished.[6]

Colonists endured disease and starvation during the Starving Time.

John Rolfe helped make tobacco a successful cash crop in Virginia.

JOHN ROLFE
AND POCAHONTAS

amestown had been built on swampy
ground and was full of disease-carrying
mosquitoes. To get away from the pests, Dale moved
most of the settlement near the falls of the James
River. The area, called Henricus, was enclosed by

palisades and included large fields. As at Jamestown, the threat of attack by Native Americans kept the settlers and animals inside the palisades.

While many settlers moved to Henricus, others remained at Jamestown, including John Rolfe. He had sailed for Virginia in 1609 on the *Sea Venture* and was wrecked on Bermuda. Rolfe spent several months there while small boats were built from the wreckage so that the voyage could continue. Rolfe's wife and child were with him on Bermuda. However, his child died before the ships could be repaired.

When Rolfe finally reached Virginia, the situation was grim. The settlers were in terrible shape. They had grown very little food, and the local Native Americans were attacking. Disease continued to spread throughout the colony. Rolfe's wife became ill and died shortly after they reached the colony.

A New Crop

The Jamestown colonists were under pressure from the Virginia Company to produce something of value. They had not found the gold or other precious resources that had been expected, and the Virginia Company was losing money on its investments in the colony.

Rolfe had the idea that he could improve the native tobacco and sell it in England. Rolfe brought with him a type of tobacco from the West Indies. This tobacco was more pleasant than the local Indian tobacco. The native tobacco in Virginia was harsh and burned the throats of the English smokers. Rolfe introduced a sweeter tobacco plant from the Caribbean. He combined it with Virginia and West Indian tobacco. He dried the leaf to make it taste better. He also figured out how to farm this tobacco in Virginia.

Tobacco History

Native Americans had used tobacco for thousands of years before the arrival of Europeans. Native Americans had been smoking tobacco since approximately 2000 BCE. The word *tobacco* is a Native American word. It comes from the word for the instrument that Native Americans used to smoke it.

A Frenchman named Jean Nicot gave the plant its scientific name, *Nicotiana*. Spain had a monopoly on tobacco and was earning huge profits. In 1606, the Spanish government said any Spaniards selling tobacco plants or seeds to foreigners could be put to death.

Nonetheless, John Rolfe was able to smuggle seeds of the Caribbean strain to Virginia. Rolfe used a variety of tobacco called *Nicotiana tabacum* from Venezuela and Trinidad. This replaced the harsh tobacco native to Virginia, *Nicotiana rustica*. With this new crop of pleasing tobacco available for farming, Virginia became a prominent exporter of tobacco. Plantations spread across the South, increasing the demand for cheap labor, such as indentured servants. Plantation farming and the need for cheap labor eventually made slavery popular in the colonies.

Tobacco remained the economic base of the South until it was replaced by cotton in approximately 1800.

Rolfe made his first tobacco shipments to London in 1614. The new tobacco was popular in England, and it became the Jamestown settlement's main cash crop. Four years later, in 1618, Virginia was shipping 50,000 pounds (22,680 kg) of tobacco to England annually. Indentured servants were later brought to Virginia to work the increasing number of tobacco plantations.

Pocahontas Is Captured

Pocahontas had not been in contact with the colonists since John Smith had returned to England. On April, 13, 1614, Samuel Argall, an English sea captain who had been charged with the job of finding the Northwest Passage, kidnapped Pocahontas. He lured her onto his ship and then refused to release her. The colonists told the Powhatan they wanted to exchange Pocahontas for English prisoners, food, and tools the Native Americans had taken. Argall brought Pocahontas to Jamestown and held her captive. Powhatan agreed to return the prisoners and provide corn, but refused to return the tools.

When the settlers received only part of the ransom they demanded, they took Pocahontas and marched on the Powhatan settlement. The colonists

Samuel Argall kidnapped Pocahontas.

intended to take the rest of the ransom by force. Fighting erupted. The Native Americans attacked the colonists. The English burned houses and killed several warriors.

After the fight, Pocahontas met two of her brothers. She told them that she had received good treatment. Later, Pocahontas moved to Henricus. She received Christian religious instruction under the Reverend Alexander Whitaker. She also learned to read the Bible and to write.

It was not long before she and John Rolfe, a religious man, began to spend time together. In time, their friendship turned into a romantic relationship. According to one colonist, Raphe Hamor, it had become clear that "their contact resulted in Rolfe falling in love with [Pocahontas] and she with him."[1]

Rolfe was a religious man and seemed to love Pocahontas. But it was not until after she continued her Christian studies and was baptized (taking the Christian name Rebecca) that he asked her to marry him. Rolfe then spoke with Thomas Dale, the current governor of Virginia, requesting permission to marry Pocahontas. Dale agreed that marriage would be appropriate.

Pocahontas's father, Chief Powhatan, also agreed to the marriage. He sent two of his sons to witness the occasion. The English were happy at the prospect of a cross-

Rolfe's Claim

Although many historians believe that John Rolfe loved Pocahontas, he claimed he wanted to marry Pocahontas not to satisfy himself but rather "for the good of this plantation for the honour of our [country], for the glory of God, for my [own] salvation, and for the converting to the true knowledge of God and Jesus Christ, an [unbelieving] creature, namely [Pocahontas]."[2]

cultural marriage between Rolfe, an important
figure in the Jamestown colony, and Pocahontas, the
daughter of paramount Chief Powhatan. They hoped
that the marriage would improve relations with the
Powhatan. Rolfe and Pocahontas married on
April 5, 1614. ⌒

The marriage of Pocahontas and John Rolfe

Ætatis suæ 21. A. 1616.

Pocahontas wearing English clothing

The Colonists Thrive

For a while, the union between the Powhatan and the English helped ease their relations. The peace allowed Jamestown to grow and the settlers to prosper. As Jamestown settler Raphe Hamor described it:

Ever since [the marriage of Pocahontas and John Rolfe] we have had friendly commerce and trade, not [only] with Powhatan [himself], but also with his subjects round about us; so as now I see no reason why the [Colony] should not thrive.[1]

The period from the marriage of Pocahontas and Rolfe until her death is sometimes called the "Peace of Pocahontas."

Jamestown continued to expand. John Rolfe listed several "suburbs" of Jamestown: Henricus (38 men), Bermuda Nether Hundred (119 men), West and Sherley Hundred (25 men), James Towne (50 men), Kequoghtan (20 men), and Dales Gifte (17 men).

POCAHONTAS IN ENGLAND

The Virginia Company of London was always looking for good advertising. By showing its success to the public in England, they hoped to attract more investors. The conversion of Pocahontas to Christianity and her marriage to

Indentured Servitude

As the number of plantations in Virginia increased, so did the need for workers. Many thousands of indentured servants sailed to Jamestown. If they completed their seven years' labor, they might even receive land, as well as freedom. However, the servants were not always treated well and their masters could use them in almost any way they saw fit. The captain of one ship noted that servants were bought and sold much like animals.

Rolfe provided a prime opportunity for the Virginia Company. Her conversion showed that the Virginia Company was meeting its goals in Jamestown, which included fostering good relations with the Native Americans and bringing them to Christianity.

In early 1616, Virginia Governor Thomas Dale traveled to London with John Rolfe, Pocahontas, and their son Thomas. Ten other Native Americans were included in the tour as well. They met the king, the royals, and other notable people in English high society.

On her trip to England, Pocahontas also met with John Smith, whom she had not seen for

Advertising the Virginia Colony

The Virginia Company was always looking for ways to promote the company and gain investors. They were also looking for more people to move to the colony and grow tobacco for export. To lure people to live in Virginia, the Virginia Company periodically published pamphlets about the colony. Essentially, these were advertisements that pointed out the colony's better points while ignoring the negatives. For example, one pamphlet called the colony a paradise. The advertisement went on to say that the Virginia Colony

is also commendable and [hopeful] in every way, the [air] and [climate] most [sweet] and [wholesome], much warmer then England, and very agreeable to our Natures.[2]

The pamphlet continued to list all the animals, good waters, and easy living to be had in this paradise. It added, ". . . what may we hope, when [Art] and Nature both shall [join], and strive together, to give best content to man and beast?"[3]

approximately eight years. She was shocked to learn he was alive. After Smith left Jamestown, the settlers had told Pocahontas that he had died.

In March 1617, Rolfe returned to Virginia. As the group was preparing to leave, both Thomas and Pocahontas became ill, possibly with pneumonia or tuberculosis. She told her husband, "All must die. 'Tis enough that the child liveth."[4]

According to historian Benjamin Woolley, "All hopes of her recovery now rested either on the purging and blood-letting of English physicians, or the 'extreme howling, shouting, singing, and . . . violent gestures, and Antic actions'"performed by Indian priests who had been brought to London.[5]

Despite all efforts, Pocahontas died and was buried in England. Thomas remained in England with Rolfe's relatives to recover. Rolfe returned alone to Virginia, without his beloved wife and never to see his son again.

Meeting John Smith

Some people who witnessed the meeting of Pocahontas and John Smith thought that her troubled reaction revealed her undying love for Smith. However, according to Chief Roy Crazy Horse, of the Powhatan Renape Nation, "She was so furious with [Smith] that she turned her back to him, hid her face, and went off by herself for several hours. Later, in a second encounter, she called him a liar and showed him the door."[6] This was their last meeting.

SPREAD OF THE COLONY

In 1618, Chief Powhatan died, and his brother, Opechancanough, became leader. Opechancanough told the English that the peace his brother had begun would continue between their peoples. However, the English did not respect Powhatan territory and continued to push farther into it. In time, Opechancanough lost patience trying to cooperate with the settlers. He came to view them as invaders and was determined get rid of them.

That same year, the Virginia Company decided to make the laws governing the colony more like the laws in England. In April 1619, George Yeardley traveled to Jamestown as the last Virginia Company governor. He intended to help the settlers with elections. Yeardley canceled Dale's harsh laws and set up a "general assembly" in which the members would be elected by the settlers. Although only landowning men could vote, Jamestown held its first democratic election. Twenty-two men were elected into the House of Burgesses, the first representative government in North America. On July 30, 1619,

Cause of Death

Benjamin Woolley, a British historian, believes that the poor London air may have had something to do with Pocahontas becoming ill. According to Woolley, Pocahontas, "was choked in pollution, from coal fires, the [fetid] river Fleet, and [neighboring] Smithfield, a huge cattle market . . . [known for its] putrid smells."[7]

they met for the first time in the Jamestown church to consider laws for Jamestown.

In 1619, the Virginia Company started a Maids for Virginia program. More than 140 high-ranking women were sent to Jamestown. The Virginia Company hoped that the women would marry wealthy gentlemen and encourage them to stay in Jamestown. However, if a man wanted to marry one of these women, he had to pay 150 pounds (68 kg) of tobacco to the company. Thus, Maids for Virginia was another moneymaking venture for the Virginia Company.

The Virginia Company experienced a great increase in profits with the sale of Virginia tobacco. To encourage even more tobacco farming, they began to give land to former indentured servants who had completed their contracts. Wealthy people also were allowed to buy more land. The Virginia Company introduced land reforms that allowed farmers to purchase land more easily. They began to spread out

Women in Jamestown

As more women began to arrive in Jamestown they also began to have more influence on the settlement's activities. One of their primary roles was to provide stability to the colony. They did this by establishing families. Lord Bacon, a member of the British parliament, wrote that to make a place self-sustaining, "it is time to plant with women as well as with men; that the plantation may spread into generations, and not be ever pieced from without."[8]

so they could acquire more Powhatan land and grow more tobacco. Farmers started large tobacco-growing farms called plantations.

Another "program" started in 1619 brought Africans to work the plantations. This was the beginning of African labor in America. Twenty Africans arrived on a ship called *St. John the Baptist* from the area of modern Angola, in southwest Africa. The captives were en route to the Mexican coast. However, a Dutch ship captured them and took them to Jamestown. The Dutch traded the Africans for food and drink. Initially, the Africans were indentured servants, but their presence in Jamestown paved the way for race-based slavery.

The Jamestown settlement was firmly established by this point. It was clear to the Powhatan that the Jamestown settlement was growing and establishing itself more fully. The Powhatan and English had worked and lived side by side for more than ten years. They had married one another and lived in one another's towns. There were more and longer periods of peace. But as the settlers grew in number, the two groups again began to isolate themselves from one another. Suspicion and hostility increased.

African slaves arrived in Virginia in the 1600s.

Colonists under attack from Powhatan Indians

THE POWHATAN RESIST

he Peace of Pocahontas had lasted several years. After her death in 1617, the peace evaporated. In 1618, the Virginia Company provided funds to the colony to educate, civilize, and Christianize the Native Americans. The Virginia

Company intended to integrate them into the English society of Jamestown. The Virginia Company and its investors believed that the Native Americans should become peaceful Christian farmers. They wanted to educate the Native Americans like English children.

The investors in the Virginia Company hoped that once the Native Americans had integrated into English society, the fighting between the two cultures would end. Then, more English people would be willing to go to Virginia and establish other colonies and plantations.

However, the Native Americans had not agreed to the idea of integration. They viewed the prospect of integration into English society as cultural suicide. Most Native Americans were unwilling to lose their cultural identity at the request of the English.

PLAN OF ATTACK

Opechancanough was growing restless. More English settlers continued to arrive in Jamestown.

A School for Native Americans

By 1621, George Thorpe, a settler from London, had attempted to establish a school for Native American children. The school would teach them to read, write, and become Christians. London donors generously gave money to get the school under way. When Opechancanough led an attack against the settlers in 1622, Thorpe was one of those who died. The hope for the school died with him.

The settlers continued to spread out and take over Powhatan lands. On March 21, 1622, the Powhatan visited Jamestown and the outlying settlements. Robert Beverley, an English eyewitness, wrote, "they brought presents of deer, turkeys, fish, and fruits. . . ."[1]

On March 22, the Powhatan returned to the settlement and the unsuspecting English. Opechancanough had instructed his people to take the tools belonging to the English and to kill as many settlers as possible. Beverley added:

> *The very morning of the massacre they came freely and unarmed among them, eating with them and behaving themselves with the same freedom and friend-ship as formerly till the very minute they were to put their plot in execution. Then they fell to work all at once everywhere, knock-ing the English unawares on the head, some with their hatchets, which they call tomahawks, others with the hoes and axes of the English themselves, shooting at those who escaped the reach of their hands, sparing neither age nor sex but destroying man, woman, and child.[2]*

The Powhatan killed 347 settlers in the settlements outside the Jamestown fort. They burned homes and workshops. When they destroyed the settlers' crops and fields, they destroyed the food that would take the settlers through the winter.

Opechancanough also had planned to destroy the Jamestown fort and kill the colonists within. A young Native American boy named Canco, however, warned those settlers. They were able to hide behind their fort walls and defend themselves.

After the attack, the settlers were too frightened to leave the fort and return to their homes and farms. No food could be grown or harvested. Those who had survived the attacks on the outlying settlements flooded the fort, straining food supplies even more.

Conditions became as bad as they had been when the settlement was first established. Settlers became sick. Supply ships from England also carried disease. Approximately 400 settlers died that winter of disease and starvation.

Placing the Blame

Thorpe, one of the settlers killed in the attack, was sympathetic to the situation the Native Americans were in. About a year before the attack, he had written that, as Christians, the colonists should have been more charitable to the Native Americans. He also considered the Native Americans to have a peaceful and virtuous disposition.

RETALIATION

When news of the Native American attacks reached London in May 1622, the Virginia Company took a different view on integrating the Powhatan into the English culture of Jamestown. After the attacks, their only discussion was whether to kill the Native Americans or enslave them. The Virginia Company decided that the English would fight back. They decided on war.

The Virginia Company sent groups of military men to Virginia, and they began to attack Native American settlements. Settler Edward Waterhouse wrote that the English intended to

---

How the Jamestown Fort Was Saved

Colonist Edward Waterhouse wrote a letter in 1622 describing how Jamestown was saved. A young Native American who lived with an English family learned about the coming attack. He warned the settlers in Jamestown. Waterhouse wrote:

That the slaughter had [been universal], if God had not put it into the heart of an Indian belonging to one Perry, to disclose it . . . Perries Indian rose out of his bed and [explained] it to Pace . . . And thus the rest of the Colony that had warning [given] them, by this [means] was [saved]. . . .

Pace [upon] this [discovery], securing his house, before day rowed [over the river] to [Jamestown] (in that place [near] three miles [across]) and [gave] notice thereof to the [Governor], by which [means] they were [prevented] there, and at such other Plantations as was possible for a timely intelligence to be [given]; for where they saw [us] standing [upon] our Guard, at the sight of a [gun] they all [ran] away.[3]

"invade the country, and destroy [those] who sought to destroy us."[4]

The English military copied the Powhatan tactics and pretended to be friendly before attacking. They allowed the Native Americans to plant their crops. Then the English burned the crops just before harvest. Groups of armed Englishmen killed individual Powhatan and entire towns of Native Americans, wherever they found them.

A group of Englishmen were invited by the Powhatan to discuss peace. After accepting their kindness and eating their food, the English poisoned the drinks of as many Powhatan as possible. The poisoning killed 200 Powhatan. The English then murdered approximately 50 of the surviving Powhatan.

COLLAPSE OF THE VIRGINIA COMPANY

Indian attacks continued at Jamestown, killing settlers and destroying property. In return, the English continued their retaliatory attacks. In these warlike conditions, crops were destroyed or neglected and the profits for the Virginia Company plummeted. It did not take long before the Virginia Company began losing money.

The English government began to investigate mismanagement among the Virginia Company's leaders. In 1624, the Virginia Company collapsed. King James I revoked the company's charter and took direct control of Virginia as a royal colony. Far from being the end of Jamestown, this action provided yet another new beginning for the colony.

Conditions in Virginia

The major problem of the Jamestown colony was the lack of food. However, overcrowding was also a problem. Many colonists blamed the colony's leaders for privately complaining about poor conditions. But in letters to the Virginia Company in London, the same leaders spoke "for the most part all good, [giving] assurance of [abundance] and [prosperity]." This practice, according to one colonist, lured thousands of people to come to Jamestown, "seduced with the hope [only] of an [imaginary] plenty."[5]

The appropriately named New Town was laid out to the east of the fort. Tobacco fueled the growing economy. In the coming years, many new settlers arrived. Jamestown became the colony's capital and an important English port in America.

By the 1640s, the Virginia colonists had settled into a fairly normal pattern of life. The settlers were better able to support themselves, and the threat of starvation faded.

The Powhatan were still alarmed, however, at the colony's growth. On April 17, 1644, Opechancanough launched a surprise attack against the settlers. His people killed

The colonists captured Chief Opechancanough and held him prisoner.

about 500 men, women, and children. However, Opechancanough could not defeat the English. He was captured by the English and held prisoner. A soldier guarding him murdered him while he was in custody.

After Openchancanough's death, the Powhatan were forced to sign a treaty that moved them to the middle of the peninsula of Virginia to a reservation on the Pamunkey River. The publication *Notable Native Americans* notes, "[T]he area north of the Pamunkey River and south of the Rappahannock was 'forever' reserved to the Native Americans. Forever, in this case, lasted for three years."[6]

In 1649, the Virginia government opened land for settlement that had belonged to the Powhatan. This sort of treaty making and breaking set a pattern for U.S. relations with Native Americans. The pattern lasted well into the twentieth century and affected every native group on the continent.

The Powhatan Indians signed a treaty, which moved them
to a reservation on the Pamunkey River.

Many buildings in Jamestown were destroyed during Bacon's Rebellion.

THE FALL OF JAMESTOWN

hroughout the early 1670s, English settlers continued to attack their Native American neighbors. Finally, the Powhatan were forced to sign a peace treaty with the English. As part of the treaty, they received a reservation. This land set apart for Powhatan use was given in return for a yearly payment to the Virginia governor. In return for the land, the Powhatan were required to pay a small tribute of beaver skins every year to the capital.

Jamestown experienced many setbacks. In 1676, a group of Virginia colonists revolted against the colony's government. They felt that the governor, William Berkeley, was doing nothing to end the Native American attacks on English settlements. Nathaniel Bacon, a planter, led the revolt, which is commonly known today as Bacon's Rebellion. The colonial capital was burned to the ground in the revolt.

By the 1690s, not many people remained in Jamestown. Most people had left to live in other parts of Virginia. In 1698, many of the remaining buildings in Jamestown burned. After the fire, the capital of the colony was moved permanently from Jamestown to Williamsburg. Most of the buildings in Jamestown were abandoned and left to rot.

Though the site was later used during the Revolutionary War and

Native Americans in Virginia Today

Since 1983, the commonwealth of Virginia has recognized eight Indian nations. These are the Chickahominy, Eastern Chickahominy, Mattaponi, Upper Mattaponi, Monacan, Nansemond, Pamunkey, and Rappahannock. Most, though not all, live on reservation lands.

the U.S. Civil War, the site was mostly forgotten for many years. The end of the Jamestown era had come.

FINAL REMEMBRANCE

In 1994, archaeologists discovered the site of the first Jamestown fort. The Association for the Preservation of Virginia Antiquities (APVA), along with the National Park Service, began to excavate the site. According to the APVA, "Over one million objects reflective of life at James Fort have been unearthed so far, as well as the burials of over 70 colonists including the remains of a high-ranking colonist."[1] The digs have given modern Americans a glimpse into life in the first permanent English settlement in North America.

The National Park Service manages the rest of the site, including New Town. At that site, many more artifacts from the 1600s have been revealed to modern eyes.

Williamsburg, Virginia

Settlers chose the site that became Williamsburg because it had fewer mosquitoes and better farm land than Jamestown. The site was originally called the Middle Plantation because of its location in the middle of a peninsula between the James and York rivers. Its name was changed to Williamsburg in 1699 to honor King William III of England. Williamsburg was the Virginia capital until 1780 when Richmond became the capital of Virginia. Today, historic Williamsburg is an educational tourist attraction. Guides, craft workers, and other employees dress in colonial costumes.

Archaeologists uncovered a well at the Jamestown site.

The four-hundredth anniversary of the founding of Jamestown was in 2007. Virginia Native Americans were unhappy that the founding was going to be celebrated. The only thing it had done for their ancestors, many of them believed, was end their way of life.

"You can't celebrate an invasion," stated Mary Wade, an influential Jamestown 2007

Commemoration planner and Indian activist, has stated. After all, Indian tribes "were pushed back off of their land, even killed. Whole tribes were annihilated. A lot of people carry that oral history with them, and that's why they use the word 'invasion,' because it truly was an invasion, and I'm sure some of the Indian people will probably want to tell that as a part of the story of 400 years."[2]

Instead of being celebrated, the event was simply remembered. People remembered both the English and the Powhatan. The story of Jamestown is about new beginnings— for the town and for the people who came to Virginia from foreign shores.

Association for the Preservation of Virginia Antiquities

The Association for the Preservation of Virginia Antiquities (APVA) was founded in 1889. Its original purpose was to save Jamestown. Today, APVA administers more than 20 properties to preserve Virginia's history and educate the public. Six of its properties are on the list of National Historic Landmarks.

The Jamestown excavation site

Timeline

1492	1584	1587
Christopher Columbus arrives in the Caribbean islands in the fall.	Queen Elizabeth I gives Walter Raleigh permission to establish a colony in North America.	Colonists land on Roanoke Island on July 22.

1607	1607	1607
Powhatan Indians attack the settlers for the first time on May 26.	A long-term drought affects the area around Jamestown.	John Smith and companions explore the Chesapeake Bay in December. Smith is captured and meets Chief Powhatan.

1603	1606	1607
James VI of Scotland becomes king of England.	The Virginia Company is chartered.	Three Virginia Company ships enter Chesapeake Bay on April 26.

1608	1608	1609
The First Supply arrives at Jamestown on January 2.	Christopher Newport arrives at Jamestown with the Second Supply in September.	The Third Supply arrives at Jamestown on August 11. The *Sea Venture* is shipwrecked in Bermuda.

TIMELINE

1609	1609	1610
Newport leaves Jamestown for London in the fall. George Percy takes control of Jamestown.	The Starving Time begins in the winter and kills most of the Jamestown settlers within the year.	The *Sea Venture* lands at Jamestown in the spring. John Rolfe arrives. Thomas Gates enacts harsh laws.

1618	1619	1622
Powhatan dies in April. His brother Opechancanough becomes chief.	George Yeardley institutes a general assembly and sets up the first democratic elections in North America.	Opechancanough leads an attack to drive the English out of Virginia on March 22.

1611	1614	1616
Thomas Dale becomes the Jamestown leader on May 12.	Rolfe ships the first of his new tobacco back to England.	Pocahontas travels to England. She dies there in March 1617.

1646	1676	1698
The Powhatan sign a peace treaty with the English.	Nathaniel Bacon leads a rebellion against the Virginia governor.	Many remaining buildings in Jamestown burn. The Virginia capital is moved to Williamsburg.

ESSENTIAL FACTS

DATE OF EVENT

1607–1698

PLACE OF EVENT

Jamestown and surrounding areas, English colony of Virginia

KEY PLAYERS

- ❖ Elizabeth I, queen of England
- ❖ James I, king of England after Elizabeth died
- ❖ Captain John Smith, leader of the Jamestown colony
- ❖ Paramount Chief Powhatan, most powerful leader of the Powhatan
- ❖ Christopher Newport, commander of many supply ships to Jamestown
- ❖ Opechancanough, brother of Powhatan
- ❖ Pocahontas, daughter of Powhatan
- ❖ John Rolfe, husband of Pocahontas and developer of tobacco as cash crop

Highlights of Event

- ❖ In 1606, James I gave permission to the Virginia Company of London to establish colonies in Virginia.
- ❖ The first English colonists landed on an island on the coast of Virginia on May 14, 1607. They named the settlement Jamestown.
- ❖ Opechancanough captured John Smith in December 1607 and took him to meet the powerful paramount Chief Powhatan.
- ❖ During the winter of 1609 to 1610, the Starving Time killed most of the settlers at Jamestown.
- ❖ John Rolfe arrived in Jamestown in spring 1610. He developed a new strain of tobacco that became popular in England. The tobacco industry saved Jamestown.
- ❖ The Powhatan signed a peace treaty with the English and gave up most of their traditional lands.
- ❖ After a fire in Jamestown, the colonial capital of Virginia was moved to Williamsburg. This ended the Jamestown era.

Quote

"In honour of their King, the council dutifully called this ramshackle collection of tents pitched on a sweaty island in the middle of a teeming forest 'Jamestown.'" —*Benjamin Woolley*, Savage Kingdom

ADDITIONAL RESOURCES

SELECT BIBLIOGRAPHY

Association for the Preservation of Virginia Antiquities (APVA). *Jamestown Rediscovery*. http://www.apva.org/jr.html.

Horn, James. *A Land as God Made It: Jamestown and the Birth of America*. New York: Basic Books, 2005.

Lange, Karen E. *1607: A New Look at Jamestown*. Washington, DC: National Geographic Society, 2007.

Woolley, Benjamin. *Savage Kingdom: The True Story of Jamestown, 1607, and the Settlement of America*. New York: HarperCollins, 2007.

FURTHER READING

Cooper, Michael L. *Jamestown, 1607*. New York: Holiday House, 2007.

Karwoski, Gail. *Miracle: The True Story of the Wreck of the Sea Venture*. Plain City, OH: Darby Creek, 2004.

Riehecky, Janet. *The Settling of Jamestown*. Milwaukee, WI: World Almanac Library, 2002.

Web Links

To learn more about Jamestown, visit ABDO Publishing Company online at **www.abdopublishing.com**. Web sites about Jamestown are featured on our Book Links page. These links are routinely monitored and updated to provide the most current information available.

Places to Visit

Colonial National Historic Park

Colonial National Historical Pkwy, Uninc James City County, VA
757-229-1733
www.nps.gov/colo
See the historic sites including the Cape Henry Memorial, historic Jamestown, and Yorktown.

Jamestown Settlement

2218 Jamestown Road, Route 31 South, Williamsburg, VA 23185
888-593-4682
www.historicjamestowne.org/index.php
Visit the site of the original Jamestown settlement and learn how the settlers built Jamestown.

National Museum of the American Indian

Smithsonian Institution
Fourth Street and Independence Avenue Southwest, Washington, DC 20560
202-633-1000
www.nmai.si.edu
View artifacts from Native American tribes and see exhibits on Native American culture.

GLOSSARY

adventurer
    An investor in the Virginia Company.

Bermuda
    A group of islands in the Atlantic Ocean.

charter
    Permission from the king or queen to start a colony.

governing council
    The group of men who were to administer Jamestown.

House of Burgesses
    The first elected government of Virginia and in North America.

indentured servant
    Someone who worked unpaid for up to seven years in return for passage to a new place and training in a trade.

militia
    A group of armed civilians who train together as a military unit.

New World
    Another name for North, South, and Central America.

Northwest Passage
    A legendary water shortcut across North America connecting the Atlantic and Pacific oceans.

palisade
    Tall posts placed upright in the ground to form a protective wall.

paramount chief
    Most powerful leader of the Powhatan.

Peace of Pocahontas
    The period from 1614, when Pocahontas married John Rolfe, until 1617, when she died.

Pilgrim
    Puritans or Separatists who left England for religious reasons and began a colony in Massachusetts.

plantation
> A large tobacco-growing farm.

Renape
> The Powhatan name for themselves, meaning "human beings."

Spanish Armada
> A large fleet of Spanish warships that attempted to invade England in 1588.

Tidewater
> The part of Virginia lying between the Atlantic Coast and the first waterfalls on inland rivers to the west.

Treaty of Tordesillas
> An agreement that divided the known world between Spain and Portugal.

Virginia Company of London
> A group of investors who organized and sent the colonists to Jamestown; also called the Virginia Company.

werowance
> A Powhatan leader.

SOURCE NOTES

Chapter 1. A New Way of Life
1. William Shakespeare. *The Tempest*. Act 5, Scene 1. 1 Dec. 2007
<http://etext.virginia.edu/etcbin/toccer-new2?id=MobTemp.
sgm&images=images/modeng&data=/texts/english/modeng/parsed&tag=p
ublic&part=5&division=div1>.
2. Karen E. Lange. *1607: A New Look at Jamestown*. Washington, DC:
National Geographic Society, 2007. 44.
3. Ibid.
4. Ibid.

Chapter 2. New Life in a New Land
1. Stephen Greenblatt. "Raleigh, Sir Walter." World Book Online
Reference Center. 2007. 6 Dec. 2007 <http://www.worldbookonline.
com/wb/Article?id=ar458740>.
2. Richard Hakluyt. *Principal Navigations: Voyages of the English Nation*, vol. 3
(1600). 27 Nov. 2007 <http://personal.pitnet.net/primarysources/
ronoake.html>.
3. John White. "The Fifth Voyage of M. John White into the West
Indies and Parts of America Called Virginia, in the Yeere 1590."
Virtual Jamestown, Virginia Center for Digital History, University of
Virginia. 30 Nov. 2007 <http://etext.lib.virginia.edu/etcbin/jamestown-
browse?id=J1019>.

Chapter 3. Reaching Virginia
1. Avalon Law Project at Yale Law School. "The First Charter of Virginia;
April 10, 1606." 6 Dec. 2007 <http://www.yale.edu/lawweb/avalon/states/
va01.htm>.
2. William Strachey. *A True Reportory of the Wreck and Redemption of Sir Thomas Gates,
Knight, upon and from the Islands of the Bermudas: His Coming to Virginia and the Estate
of that Colony Then and After, under the Government of the Lord La Warr, July 15, 1610*.
Virtual Jamestown, Virginia Center for Digital History, University of
Virginia. 2. 4 Dec. 2007. <www.virtualjamestown.org/TR%20modern.
doc>.
3. Michael L. Cooper. *Jamestown, 1607*. New York: Holiday House, 2007.
16.
4. "Christopher Newport." *Dictionary of American Biography* Base Set. American
Council of Learned Societies, 1928–1936. *Biography Resource Center*.
Farmington Hills, MI: Thomson Gale. 2007. 7 Dec. 2007. <http://0-
galenet.galegroup.com.libraryapp.carverlib.org:80/servlet/BioRC>.
5. Benjamin Woolley. *Savage Kingdom: The True Story of Jamestown, 1607, and the
Settlement of America*. New York: HarperCollins, 2007. 65.

Chapter 4. Misunderstandings

1. Karen E. Lange. *1607: A New Look at Jamestown*. Washington, DC: National Geographic Society, 2007. 14.
2. Roy Crazy Horse. "Powhatan History in the Words of Chief Roy Crazy Horse." 28 Nov. 2007 <http://www.powhatan.org/history.html>.
3. Benjamin Woolley. *Savage Kingdom: The True Story of Jamestown, 1607, and the Settlement of America*. New York: HarperCollins, 2007. 74.
4. Ibid.
5. Karen E. Lange. *1607: A New Look at Jamestown*. Washington, DC: National Geographic Society, 2007. 27.
6. Ibid. 28.
7. Dennis B. Blanton. "Jamestown's Environment." Virtual Jamestown, Virginia Center for Digital History, University of Virginia. 30 Nov. 2007 <http://www.virtualjamestown.org/essays/blanton_essay.html>.
8. Edward Maria Wingfield. "A Discourse of Virginia." Charles Deane, ed. Virtual Jamestown, Virginia Center for Digital History, University of Virginia. 6 Dec. 2007 <http://etext.lib.virginia.edu/etcbin/jamestown-browsemod?id=J1023>.

Chapter 5. The John Smith Era

1. Benjamin Woolley. *Savage Kingdom: The True Story of Jamestown, 1607, and the Settlement of America*. New York: HarperCollins, 2007. 114.
2. "Captain Smith's Relation of His Being Taken Prisoner by the Indians, How They Conjured Him, Powhatan Entertained Him, Would Have Slain Him, and How His Daughter Saved His Life." Quoted in Benjamin Woolley. *Savage Kingdom: The True Story of Jamestown, 1607, and the Settlement of America*. New York: HarperCollins, 2007. 123.
3. John White. "The True Pictures and Fashions of the People in That Part of America Now Called Virginia." Virtual Jamestown, Virginia Center for Digital History, University of Virginia. 6 Dec. 2007 <http://etext.lib.virginia.edu/etcbin/jamestown-browse?id=J1009b>.
4. Karen E. Lange. *1607: A New Look at Jamestown*. Washington, DC: National Geographic Society, 2007. 29.
5. Roy Crazy Horse. "The Pocahontas Myth." 28 Nov. 2007 <http://www.powhatan.org/pocc.html>.
6. Karen E. Lange. *1607: A New Look at Jamestown*. Washington, DC: National Geographic Society, 2007. 28.
7. Association for the Preservation of Virginia Antiquities (APVA). *A Timeline of Events and References Leading Up to and Through the Founding of Jamestown*. 5 Nov. 2007 <www.apva.org/history/timeline.html>.

Source Notes Continued

8. Association for the Preservation of Virginia Antiquities (APVA). *Captain John Smith*. 5 Nov. 2007 <www.apva.org/history/jsmith.html>.

Chapter 6. The Starving Time

1. Benjamin Woolley. *Savage Kingdom: The True Story of Jamestown, 1607, and the Settlement of America*. New York: HarperCollins, 2007. 228.
2. William Strachey. *A True Reportory of the Wreck and Redemption of Sir Thomas Gates, Knight, upon and from the Islands of the Bermudas: His Coming to Virginia and the Estate of that Colony Then and After, under the Government of the Lord La Warr, July 15, 1610.* Virtual Jamestown, Virginia Center for Digital History, University of Virginia. 4 Dec. 2007 <www.virtualjamestown.org/TR%20modern.doc>.
3. Karen E. Lange. *1607: A New Look at Jamestown*. Washington, DC: National Geographic Society, 2007. 31.
4. William Strachey. *A True Reportory of the Wreck and Redemption of Sir Thomas Gates, Knight, upon and from the Islands of the Bermudas: His Coming to Virginia and the Estate of that Colony Then and After, under the Government of the Lord La Warr, July 15, 1610.* Virtual Jamestown, Virginia Center for Digital History, University of Virginia. 4 Dec. 2007 <www.virtualjamestown.org/TR%20modern.doc>.
5. Association for the Preservation of Virginia Antiquities (APVA). *A Timeline of Events and References Leading Up to and Through the Founding of Jamestown*. 5 Nov. 2007 <www.apva.org/history/timeline.html>.
6. "Tragical Relation of the Virginia Assembly, 1624." *Firsthand Accounts of Virginia, 1575–1705*, Virtual Jamestown, 30 Nov. 2007 <http://etext.lib. virginia.edu/etcbin/jamestown-browse?id=J1041>.

Chapter 7. John Rolfe and Pocahontas

1. Benjamin Woolley. *Savage Kingdom: The True Story of Jamestown, 1607, and the Settlement of America*. New York: HarperCollins, 2007. 316.
2. Raphe Hamor. "A True Discourse of the Present Estate of Virginia." Virtual Jamestown, Virginia Center for Digital History, University of Virginia. 30 Nov. 2007 <http://etext.lib.virginia.edu/etcbin/jamestown-browse?id=J1004>.

Chapter 8. The Colonists Thrive

1. Raphe Hamor. "A True Discourse of the Present Estate of Virginia." Virtual Jamestown, Virginia Center for Digital History, University of Virginia. 30 Nov. 2007 <http://etext.lib.virginia.edu/etcbin/jamestown-browse?id=J1004>.
2. R. I. *Nova Britannia*. From Virtual Jamestown, Virginia Center for Digital History, University of Virginia. 7 Dec. 2007 <http://etext.lib. virginia.edu/etcbin/jamestown-browsemod?id=J1051>.

3. Ibid

4. Association for the Preservation of Virginia Antiquities (APVA). "Pocahontas." 28 Nov. 2007 <www.apva.org/history/pocahont.html>.

5. Benjamin Woolley. *Savage Kingdom: The True Story of Jamestown, 1607, and the Settlement of America*. New York: HarperCollins, 2007. 345.

6. Roy Crazy Horse. "The Pocahontas Myth." 28 Nov. 2007 <http://www. powhatan.org/pocc.html>.

7. Benjamin Woolley. *Savage Kingdom: The True Story of Jamestown, 1607, and the Settlement of America*. New York: HarperCollins, 2007. 338.

8. Sandy Groves. "The Indispensable Role of Women in Virginia." Colonial National Historic Park. 6 Dec. 2007 <http://www.nps.gov/ archive/colo/Jthanout/Women.html>.

Chapter 9. The Powhatan Resist

1. Robert Beverly. "Robert Beverley's Description of the 1622 Indian Attack." Virtual Jamestown, Virginia Center for Digital History, University of Virginia. 30 Nov. 2007 <http://www.virtualjamestown. org/1622attk.html>.

2. Ibid.

3. Edward Waterhouse. "A Relation of the Barbarous Massacre, 1622." Found at the Library of Congress's American Memory, 8 Dec. 2007 <http://memory.loc.gov/learn/features/timeline/colonial/indians/ massacre.html>.

4. Karen E. Lange. *1607: A New Look at Jamestown*. Washington, DC: National Geographic Society, 2007. 41.

5. "The Miserable Condition of Virginia, 1623." Library of Congress's American Memory. 8 Dec. 2007 <http://memory.loc.gov/learn/features/ timeline/colonial/virginia/miserabl.html>.

6. *Biography Resource Center*. Farmington Hills, MI: Thomson Gale. 2007. 7 Dec. 2007 <http://0-galenet.galegroup.com.libraryapp.carverlib.org:80/ servlet/BioRC>.

Chapter 10. The Fall of Jamestown

1. Association for the Preservation of Virginia Antiquities (APVA). *"400-Year-Old Jamestown Well Preserves Environmental Data and Rare Objects*. 5 Dec. 2007 <http://www.apva.org/pressroom/press_release.php?pr_id=29>.

2. Bob Unruh. "Historic Jamestown marks 400 years since 'invasion'" *WorldNewDaily*. 8 Mar. 2008 < http://www.worldnetdaily.com/news/article. asp?ARTICLE_ID=54603 >.

INDEX

ABOUT THE AUTHOR

Charles Pederson is a consulting editor, writer, and translator. He has written for and contributed to many fiction and nonfiction publications for both children and adults. A graduate in linguistics, international relations, and German, he has traveled widely, bringing to his work an appreciation of different peoples and cultures. He lives with his family near Minneapolis, Minnesota.

PHOTO CREDITS

North Wind Picture Archives, cover, 13, 14, 19, 23, 24, 30, 33, 34, 39, 43, 44, 47, 53, 54, 60, 63, 64, 68, 71, 72, 79, 80, 87, 89, 90; Nancy Carter/North Wind Picture Archives, 6, 93; Red Line Editorial, 27; Kenneth D. Lyons/AP Images, 95